THERE IS NO MIDDLE GROUND –IN GOD'S KINGDOM

EXAMINE YOURSELF
WHO ARE YOU?

FIND OUT!

UZO ODUNUKWE

WESTBOW·
PRESS
A DIVISION OF THOMAS NELSON
& ZONDERVAN

Unless otherwise noted, all Scripture quotations are from the Holy Bible, New
King James NKJV; English Standard Version ESV; Good News Bible GNB

WestBow Press books may be ordered through booksellers or by contacting:

WestBow Press
A Division of Thomas Nelson & Zondervan
1663 Liberty Drive
Bloomington, IN 47403
www.westbowpress.com
1 (866) 928-1240

ISBN: 978-1-4908-2070-5 (sc)

Library of Congress Control Number: 2013923331

Printed in the United States of America.

WestBow Press rev. date: 07/03/2014

Contents

I dedicate this book to you, because I am aware that you are not holding this book by chance. Before you were conceived in your mother's womb, before you were born, God has ordained it, that by this moment in your life, this book will be in your hand; for a particular purpose He wants fulfilled in your life.

I am very grateful to several men of God who have touched my life and helped me learn and gain insight into the living word. I thank God for the Holy Spirit, Who teaches me, and continues to guide and counsel me. May this book be of immense spiritual benefit to you, as we continue to run the race for God's Kingdom.

Acknowledgements

I wish to thank my beloved wife, Dr. Nkiruka, who during my recuperation from a major surgery motivated and encouraged me to write this book, never to allow what God has deposited in me, not to benefit others. I thank God for her patience and understanding during my late nights writing. I would also like to say thanks to my daughter Nkiru and Pastor Emma-Fred Uzoigwe for their editorial inputs, and to my elder sister Mrs. Chinwe Enemchukwu, for reading through some of the chapters. I wish to finally thank Mr. Joshua Omotosho, and my maternal cousin Mr Fred Okoye, who through their ministration, I came to Christ.

Introduction

In things of the world it is always a little to the left and a little to the right, which is a strategy in man's craftiness not to be caught on the wrong side. It has always been said that in politics, there are no permanent friends and no permanent enemies. It is a marriage of convenience. Most often, in order not to lose out completely the parties would enter into a compromise: either an alliance or what some call an accord. However, in God's kingdom it is either you are on the left or on the right; there is no middle ground. You are either hot or cold; if lukewarm, you will be spat out.

There is no compromise with God's standards, neither is there any alliance between God's kingdom and the world. Thus, you need to know who you are as a believer—using the word of God as a mirror—in order to know your state and make an informed decision of which side you will choose to be.

That is whether you will continue to carry the old wine skin, or drop it for the new; continue in the broad way or change to the narrow; whether to continue in the way that seems good in your own eye or go the way of the word of God, "which is a lamp unto our feet, and a light unto our path."

There are several lifestyle battles one will fight and win in order to make the kingdom of God; let your lifestyle not be an impediment!

As you read, may the good Lord open your heart, to understand the truth and give you the moral courage to cross over to the right side, where you will find rest, as promised by our Lord and Savior Jesus Christ.

CHAPTER I

How Great Are You?

What shall it profit a man if he gains the whole
world and lose his soul
—*Matthew 16:26*

My English teacher in secondary school always admonished us to focus on our academics—which was the main reason we were in school—rather than party. He ended up impressing this quote: "It is better to die once and live forever than to live once and die forever." For over thirty-five years since I left school this quote has been a recurring theme in the affairs of my life, especially when I have been confronted with certain major decisions.

My English teacher's quote became especially helpful when I faced decisions that could make or mar the rest of my life; decisions for which the outcomes were mutually exclusive, thus becoming irreversible regardless of the direction I took. The irreversibility of the final outcome is always a major input for the wise when making a decision or making up one's mind about a situation.

This comes in to play when we make up our minds on how to relate with God or to decide, as there are some who question it, whether there is a God. The way you choose to relate to God—or the reasoning that led you to conclude there is no God—is influenced by how great you think you are.

One tends to forget that neither a man's greatness nor his possessions can save him from death. He will still die like an animal or a mad man, as stated in Psalm 49. Regardless of whether he dies in an air-conditioned room, on a waterbed with golden frames and he is buried in a marble grave or he drowns in the ocean and his corpse is not found, it does not matter. The common denominator is that there is no more life in him. No matter how loved by anyone, he will not cohabit with the living, even if his drowned body is recovered. His corpse must be disposed of to avoid polluting the environment.

The disposal, which we call burial, requires only a small portion of ground because the living don't want to waste much land on dumping the manure of the dead body. Thus man cannot take his greatness, his wealth, the power he wielded, or that thing which he cherished most with him to his grave. If a man is satisfied with his life, if he is praised because he was a philanthropist and successful in man's eye, is God satisfied with that life? Nothing is hidden before Him.

Man may enjoy as many as seventy or more effective years in this world filled with violence, fear, injustice, cruelty, sickness, and disease. Let's imagine you are one of the richest men on earth—a philanthropist, a business tycoon, and very-kind hearted. What determines where you go after death is the decision you made in life. That decision is actually between living once and dying forever or dying once and living forever. To live once is to live one's life as one wants it, indulging the flesh and tasting the good things of this world – such as fame, power, wealth, women, and wine—without one's pivot on one's Creator, Jesus.

Your wealth or greatness cannot save you from dying because you cannot use them to pay for your life. As King David captured in Psalms 49:6—11 CEV:

> They trust in their riches and brag about all their wealth. You cannot buy back your life or pay off God! It costs far too much to buy back your life. You can never pay God enough to stay alive for ever. We see that the wise people die and so do stupid fools. Then their money is left for someone else (who they may not know). The grave will be their home forever, though they once had their own houses.

David continued in verses 13-14b:

> Here is what happens to fools and those who trust the word of fools (that there is no God or those who worship other gods): they are like sheep with death as their shepherd, leading them to the grave.

According to Scripture, the only person who can redeem you or pay God for your life so that you can live eternal life in His kingdom is Jesus Christ. The same Scripture teaches us that He is the Way, the Truth, and the Life, that no one comes to the Father except by Him.

It is unfortunate that many will find out only when it is too late, that there is hell fire in the life outside the Kingdom of God. At that stage one can do nothing to reverse their decision to refuse to come to God through Jesus. One must not try to find fulfillment where there is no fulfillment—, such as through worldly values "vanity upon vanity, all is vanity" —while neglecting the required relationship with Him. One must not busy oneself making millions, wining and dining, partying, indulging the flesh, or acquiring political or economic power and educational accolades. If a person does these, then wealth becomes their god, popularity their passion, celebrity or diva their fulfillment in life. However, humans have discovered that one cannot find fulfillment outside our Creator. Such would amount to pursuing the wind.

King Solomon (the wise king) discovered this after trying all manner of things, such as wealth, one thousand women, power, fame, and anything his heart could think of or conjure. He said in Ecclesiastes 12:13,

> "Hear the conclusion of the whole matter, fear (revere) God and keep His Commandments, for this is the whole duty of man."

CHAPTER II

Who Are You?

Jesus I know, Paul I know, who are you?
—Act 19:15

There are all manner of believers in the body of Christ, but there are only a few followers! The Scripture in 2 Timothy 2:19 tell us that God knows those who are His, and let *everyone* who names the name of the Lord God, depart from iniquity. Locate yourself as you read through the following descriptions and, if need be, judge yourself and amend your ways in order to graduate from being a believer to being a follower of Jesus. The book of Proverbs 16:25 says, "There is a way that seems good unto man, but the end leads to destruction."

These are the classes of believers.

Fast Food Believers

They are always in a hurry to leave a church service, prayer meeting, or Bible teaching. They do not go for long, drawn-out activities at the church; they want their sermons fast in order to attend to other pursuits of life or the world. You will always hear them say, "I don't have time," or "These people don't know how

5

to manage time." Most often, you find them fiddling with Cell phones, iPods, iPads, or some other distractions.

Drive-Thru Believers

They are worse than the former; they do not even come in for church meetings. They come in to register their presence, to be seen by their pastor or leaders, and then they vanish. They are always empty drums who make the most noise. They make sure they greet the leaders in the sight of others but, only stay for a few minutes of the program; or they come a few minutes to the end and make sure they greet everyone they met. Later they will be the ones expounding to those absent how great a service it was

Microwave Believers

They "microwave" the Word of God. They cram it "quick, quick," with no meditation, and then quote it verbosely in their speeches and prayers without putting the Word into practice. They take pride in memorizing but not meditating on the scriptures.

Cell phone Believers

These are the group who are busy inside the church with their phones vibrating with every text message and BB message. They surf the Internet during the service. They even text prayers to God since they do not have time for Him. They are busy, occupied with the things that give them "fulfillment". To these people their cyber-social life is more important that their eternal life.

ATM Believers

They take God as a quick dispenser of miracles, breakthroughs, and answers to prayers. Once they receive what they want, they forget God and become too busy for Him, till they need more from Him. When what they want does not happen "by fire, by force" they start complaining. Condemning others and finding faults, you see them easily changing places of worship, like rolling stones.

Laptop Believers

You see them in the church during sermons and teachings taking notes. This is very commendable, but these messages end up in that writing pad, "Random Access Memory," where they are never revisited and meditated upon to be downloaded into their hearts or hard drives, in order for the messages to impact their lives.

Facebook Believers

They are the brothers and sisters in church who spend all their time looking at others. They come to service and other church activities to look at peoples' dressings, faces, and the way others dance during praise and worship sessions. These are the things that give them fulfillment, not the Word of God or song ministrations. They end up empty after every service.

DVD Believers

These category of believers attend all Christian activities—prayer meetings, study, vigils. They hear and relay all that was said at any event without profiting from it spiritually. They are capable of giving detailed accounts of all that transpired, and they know the names of all who ministered and how powerful they are. These are believers who just go through motions.

VCD Believers

They are focused on their outward Christian lifestyle. They display all they copied and learned from their mentor preachers—their mannerisms, intonations, and patterns. Their primary focus is learning what to preach to others in order to impress, not what will impact their own lives.

Billboard Believers

They are busy advertising their church programs and inviting whoever cares, not because of passion for lost souls, but because the general overseer, pastor, or bishop, have said so, and there is a reward to it—praise or gifts or recognition.

Signboard Believers

They work like ushers and traffic wardens. They are very busy rain or shine, guiding and directing people to their church programs, but their characters are the opposite. That is, the light that beams from them will blind visitors so they can't see the way and the true light.

Satellite Believers

They are there in the church like satellites, beaming and monitoring all that is taking place in the church or Christian organization, whether or not these things are good. They then relay everything to whoever that cares or comes within their spheres. In simple terms, they are tale bearers—gossips!

Digital Believers

These are believers who are governed by the principles they believe in, their preferences, and their desires. It is either that or nothing else! No preference is given to the Word of God. Once it infringes on their comfort zones, they would rather compromise!

Celebrity Believers

They always want to be seen and recognized in the assembly of brethren, they are men and women, with all their tittles (merited & unmerited) mentioned. For instance one person could have all these titles [Rev, Dr, Evangelist, Prof, Engr, Apostle, Prophet… or His Grace, Arch Bishop "James Stow"—the Founder, General Overseer and President—Jesus Church worldwide]; they are fond of disrupting solemn assembly, prayer meetings by their presence; but before God they are nuisance, empty and have received their full reward here on earth. Whenever they are not recognized by their titles, they feel slighted.

Amplifier/Loud Speaker Believers

This category of believers are very noisy as they preach, pray, or minister; they shout at the top of their voices; as if God is not hard of hearing, nor will power be released by shouting. They assumed that they are seen as powerful preachers or prayer warriors the more they shout; but demons know those who are **HOT**! It is not by shouting. However, there is time for everything, a time to shout, and a time to forebear.

Analog Believers

These are believers who have repented, but are not converted from their old ways. They manifest all the trappings of a good Christian, but when "push" turns to be "shove" the unconverted person in them comes out. From such, one will hear "you don't know me," they will exhibit their "Old wine skin" behavior, become "carnal" and deal with the situation.

Smartphone Believers

These believers are very smart, you see them everywhere in the Church, they appear very resourceful like a pivot upon which every activity revolves, but they have hidden agendas to exploit and defraud the Church or Ministry. They 'worm' themselves into the heart of undiscerning Pastors, leaders and members and they are entrusted with responsibilities, from where they will be "milking" the Christian Organization. They are essentially the 'Judas Iscariot' in the ministry. They are so smart, that nobody will suspect them, but God knows!

Pioneer Believers

These are believers who will tell you the history of all that has happened in the local church, as they were among the "Pioneer" members. They pride themselves in comparing all the Ministers that have passed through the Church, yet their spiritual maturity can be likened to "As it was in the beginning, so it is now and it shall remain the same, until Christ comes." They are matured in Church traditions, rites, and history, but spiritually empty!

Fair Weather Believers

This category is always boisterous when things are going on well for them and they are filled with an air of "mature and faithful believer". They can be seen bouncing around like a pumped vehicle tube, but will easily leak gradually and become flat, once it gets in contact with a tiny pin! It is not difficult to know when such a believer is encountering a little hiccup in life, they will be crest-fallen and their countenance will be like that of a deflated balloon!

Churchwood believers

These are those who have imported the 'Hollywood" mentality and culture into the Church, in the name of liberty in the spirit, which they call Liberal Christianity! You can see it in their dressing, make up, choice of words, and from their liberal teachings of the word of God and preaching of accommodating Gospel. Their gospel is one that would not offend any orientation/ life style, in the name of universal love. They are quick to remind you that God is love; but are quick to forget that—God is also a Consuming Fire and God of justice.

Non-Conformist Believers

These are believers—including men of God, who manifest the gifts of the Spirit, (working of miracles, healing, prophesy, word of knowledge, discernment, etc); but are completely lacking in the manifestation of the Fruit of the Spirit; Joy, Peace, Love, Patience, Kindness, Faith, Goodness and Self-control.

Leaky Tube Believers

These believers only go to Church on Sundays to get pumped and filled by the pastor, then from Monday they start leaking little by little that by Saturday they are flat. Such cannot withstand temptation, pressures of life, etc.

Be a tube that is always filled on a constant basis. A believer who delights in the word of God, reads and meditates on the word, day and night, in line with Psalms 1:2 and Joshua 1:8, in order to observe to do such words and reap the benefits thereof. This is because such a believer understands, that God exalts His word above all His name, Psalms 38:2.

Nonaligned Believers

They are not aligned, because their character manifestation does not match what they pontificate when they preach. The way they act does not conform to the word of God; on the surface—to the unsuspecting, they seem to be wonderful men of God, but to the discerning, they are Carnal. They are self-willed, quick-tempered, and bossy; always seeking recognition at Christian gatherings or events, they would like to be noticed and recognized. These also fail to manifest the Fruit of the Spirit, Gal 5:22-23.

Prodigal Believers

These are in two categories, those who are willing to spend (Waste) money on their personal worldly wants—spending on impulse; but become frugal miserly and calculated when it comes to funding Church and Ministry projects. The other category are those who spend (waste) their time on leisure or hobbies (idols) they have passion for. They read newspapers cover to cover, watch movies, Facebook and Internet addicts—could spend 4 hours on Internet without pains. But when it comes to reading the Bible, praying, going for evangelism, attending evening programs in church, they do not have time, they feel tired, and become critical.

Cloud Believers

These are not secret disciples, like Obadiah who feared the Lord and still served in King Ahab and Queen Jezebel's cabinet, I Kings 18:3-4. They are those believers who are active inside the Church, but would never allow themselves to be identified or identify themselves by their character or utterances as followers of Christ, outside the church. They simply melt into the "Clouds of the world system" or the society rather than raise their voice in defense of their faith in Christ as occasion demands. When issues of moral values are being discussed, they lack the courage to speak out, and make contributions that would "Salt the final decision at the end of the day". They forgot that God would hold them accountable, for their lack of courage and boldness, to be the light that would shine, for others to see the true path. God 's word in Ezekiel 3:16-21, made it clear, by explaining what is required of us, as true Christians and the consequence of keeping quiet.

Align Believers

These are believers who live in consonance with the Word of God, and take reading the word seriously. They are always studying it in order to "observe to do the word", not studying to "learn what to teach others. They are filled and led by the Holy Spirit, in such a way that one can discern it. They manifest both the gifts and fruit of the Holy Spirit. They are a blessing to the body of Christ. They exercise the gift of the Spirit in love. They exude and manifest Christly character from their conduct, even under unfavorable or provocative circumstances. They have cultivated godly lifestyles; the kind that was found in Christ Jesus.

CHAPTER III

Jesus Yoke Framework

Casting all your cares upon the Lord, for He cares for you
—I Peter 5:7

Jesus gave an invitation to all those who follow Him—the invitation to yoke with him. In this timeless invitation, Jesus gave a framework for resolving problems and challenges that we face as His followers. He said,

Mathew 11:28-30:

> "Come unto me **all** you that labour and are heavy laden, and I will give you rest. Take my yoke upon you, and learn of me; for I am meek and lowly in heart; … For My yoke is easy, and my burden is light".

Seeking fulfillment or solution outside of the "yoke-burden" framework Jesus gave us is an exercise in frustration and regrets.

He emphasized "my yoke is easy, my burden is light". Instead of carrying our own heavy burden which weigh us down, to the extent of crushing the human—physically, psychologically, and spiritually—all that is required of us is to yoke with Him, learn of Him and He will give us rest; deliverance from such labour and heavy burden.

However, due to our stubborn and unbelieving human nature, some will rather believe psychics, soothsayers, unproven scientific theories, herbal/organic medicine dispensers. And without questioning, accept to take such "medications" that would eventually harm their organs; while others will not be ashamed to visit shrines and voodoo houses. Yet they find it difficult and demeaning in their own eyes, to accept the invitation from Jesus to come and yoke with Him.

To be able to accept to yoke with Him, the starting point is to humble oneself—taking His yoke upon yourself; by accepting Him into your life as your master and savior. This will create a relationship with God through Christ, now, continuing in that relationship is very vital. This continuation will enable you to be close enough to learn of Him always. This relationship will hinge on complete obedience and humility. As we continue to learn, the quickening of the word in our lives will cause our faith to grow. This is how you will start walking by faith, and the burdens that were previously described as "heavy laden" starts becoming lighter. Being sober at this stage makes it easier to study more in the word, tarry in thanksgiving, in prayers, and allowing the Holy Spirit govern our lives, which will translate, to always doing the will of God.

Jesus in the garden of Gethsemane, prayed when He was under a heavy burden (imminent death on the cross), that the cup (of the burden) be taken away, and concluded with ...... let "thy will be done"! With this statement He automatically yoked Himself with

His father, and was able to face death! By yoking with His father, He received grace and strength so He was able to bear the burden of the pain, the shame, the agony, the humiliation, the insult, and above all the sin of the whole world.

Having suffered under a heavy burden, He knows how to handle it for us—so that we will not suffer the same thing that He suffered—and emerge victorious. Therefore, yoking with Him will bring lighter burden, and victory is guaranteed! That is why, the scripture says in

Romans 8:37

> "We are more than conquerors, through Christ that loved us."

This means, in union with Christ Jesus who loved us; as we yoke with Him with the accompanying gifts and fruit of the Spirit, which will manifest easily, no amount of burden will weigh us down. Why? Because, on a constant basis they are being lifted off our shoulder by our burden bearer, Jesus.

The involvement of Holy Spirit

Partnering with the Holy Spirit is very crucial to be able to continuously yoke, and experience the light burden of our Master. Without the Holy Spirit, our Teacher, leading and guiding we tend to depend on our knowledge, wisdom and past experiences of relating with the Master. This can be likened to taking the "new wine", being offered to us, "His easy yoke and light burden", and pouring it into our own "old wine skin", of past experiences and knowledge. There will be a great burst, which may result in—backsliding or questioning "God are you there?" In our attempt to exercise our Kingdom rights of 1 Peter 5:8 "Casting all our cares (burdens) upon Him, for He careth for us" we must not approach it the wrong way; otherwise there will be no permanent rest. In all we do, we need our Helper, the Holy Spirit to get the rest promised by Master Jesus. The Holy Spirit, Whom the Master said in John 14 and 16 will lead us into all truth, is very indispensable in our moment by moment, minute by minute, week by week and year by year yoke-walking with the Lord. This is very necessary so that one is not either faster, slower, or off course! It is only the Holy Spirit, Who knows the true burden we are bearing, the frame of our minds, and also the mind of God that can help us, maintain pace with the Master.

With our limitedness, most of what we call burden based on our imaginations are not burden, but a diversion! For instance, 10 of the 12 spies that Moses sent to spy the land carried a big burden that was not there. The burden that the 10 were carrying according to the word of God was no burden at all! It was based on their negative imaginations, not based on the inspired word of God, which tells us, that we walk by faith and not by sight. Thus, they saw themselves as **Grasshoppers**, and saw their enemies as **Giants**. Every of their imagination was contrary to the word of God. They refused to yoke with God in that matter. Only Joshua and Celeb listened to the Spirit of God, and allowed Him to remind them of the promises of God concerning the matter, the whole nation would had been crushed under a non-existent burden. They automatically yoked with God, and the burden was lifted, they started seeing with the eyes of faith! Those that know their God, they see through their God. That is the major advantage of yoking with Jesus.

On the other hand, sometimes we do not have the understanding or knowledge that there is burden that is weighing us down. Also, we may know but cannot phantom what the problem is all about; the source of whatever is wrong, or how to solve it. It is only the Holy Spirit that will crack the nutty NUT! The scripture, in Romans 8:26, tells us that He (the Holy Spirit) helps our infirmity—which I call in this context our limitedness, our inadequacy of knowing what is happening to us and how to yoke with the Master. Thus He comes in and teaches us how to yoke. If we allow Him, then the promised rest is found. Without the Holy Spirit, a follower of Christ is as good as dead! That was why David in Psalm 51, cried unto God, not to take the Holy Spirit from him! The Holy Spirit in the life of the follower can be likened to water in the life of a fish!

Fish generally, cannot survive for a long time outside its natural habitat (water). Such fish would start dying gradually, but this may not be noticeable immediately. The longer it stays out the weaker it becomes, and if nothing is done to get the fish back to water, death will be the final verdict. Such fish keeps meandering, flipping up and down, and very restless. It would seem to be saying "help me relieve this "heavy burden" of living out of water"; knowing that once inside water, the yoke link with water is established, the burden lightened, and imminent death no longer a challenge. This is similar to a follower, who—knowingly or unknowingly—grieves the Holy Spirit, contrary to the charge in Ephesians 4:30 which says—*"And do not grieve the Holy Spirit of God, by whom you were sealed for the day of redemption"* NKJV, by doing things based on our own human wisdom and knowledge. If such a believer does not reconnect immediately, spiritual death is imminent! This is why we are charged in Philippians 2:12

"Work out your salvation with fear and trembling",

This requires our co-operation with the Holy Spirit.

To maintain a continuous flow with the Holy Spirit, the Word of God is very vital; reading, listening, studying, meditating, confessing and putting what we have read and meditated on into practice is very essential. This word would illuminate our path, thus revealing and unlocking the secrets and mysteries concerning any situation in our life, which has been a burden. This is in line with Psalm 119:105, which tells us that the word of God is a lamp unto our feet and a light unto our path. The above scripture clearly established that the word of God has the embedded capability, to illuminate our immediate environment and also give light to the long windy path ahead of us. So, once you yoke with Jesus—Who is the Word of God and maintain a continuous link with Him, all heavy burdens are made light, coupled with the easy yoke.

CHAPTER IV

What Is Man?

What is man that You are mindful of him,
and son of man that You visit him?
—Psalms 8:4

What is man—that in just one breath it is all over? Most humans do not realize, that each step we take as we move about, takes us (marches us) closer to our end on this earth (the grave). Also, we are not conscious of the fact that, as the clock ticks away the numberof seconds we will live on this earth reduces. These statements prompted the question above. By the time it is answered, it would reveal a lot about mans' condition in the now and in the future.

Discover who you are! Find out who God made you to be! By this I mean, you should try and get an understanding of who you are and what you are to be! I am not talking of self-discovery by occultic means. Understand how you look, what you look like, not physically, but in God's mirror. For those who said there is no God—the Atheists, Psalms 14:1 had already described them, as FOOLS!

"A fool has said in his heart, there is no God".

The real man, the man of understanding and wisdom recognizes that he was created in God's own image and likeness according to the Scriptures. Hence such a man will always strive to be what his maker wants him to be. People find it easier to believe mundane things professors teach, in subjects like History or Psychology, they are prepared to learn these things and apply them. Whereas they find it difficult, and at times belittling to believe the word of God, meditate on it and apply it by faith, to confirm whether it works. King David was not such a man, he asked God, in Psalm 8:4-8 "What is man that You are mindful of him ..." This question by David was not that of a man who is far from his creator. This means he had a good understanding of who his creator is. He knew His greatness, His awesomeness, His limitlessness, His Omnipotence- Revelations 19:6; Omniscience and Omnipresence nature – Psalms 139:4-12. He knew Him as the God, Who has the whole world in His hands. The Alpha and Omega – Revelations 21:6; the entire heaven is His throne, the clouds—the dust of His feet - Nahum 1:3b; and the earth His footstool. With all these attributes and more, when compared with man—who is just one breath away from going back to dust—David was overwhelmed with reverence. Due to lack of comparison he blurted out "What is man that You are mindful of him?" That You pay attention to him, and even visit man. The Spirit of God, gave him the answer, that man was made a little lower than the angels; that God has crowned man with glory and honour; that man had been given dominion over the works of God's hands, while God had put all things under his feet. He went ahead in verses 7-8, to enumerate such things that are under mans' feet!

However, with Adam's fall, as recorded in Genesis chapter 3, man lost his glory and honour, and his dominion over all the works of God's hands. God again, due to the fact that His lovingkindness never ceases, sent the second and last Adam to restore us back to our original position. This last Adam is Jesus Christ, as God's word states in I Corinthians 15:45-49 as follows -

".... The first man Adam became a living being." "The last Adam became a life giving spirit." However, the spiritual is not first, but the natural, and afterward the spiritual.,.. The first man was of the earth, made of dust; the second Man is the Lord (Jesus) from heaven. As was the man of dust, so also are those who are made of dust; and as is the heavenly Man, so also are those who are heavenly. And as we have borne the image of the man of dust, we shall also bear the image of the heavenly Man," NKJV.

The name Jesus, in bracket was added by me for emphasis.

Thus an unrestored man is a man of dust, very earthly in his ways and carnal; but the man who has been restored by the last Adam, is heavenly, righteous, holy and is an overcomer, as stated in Revelations 3:5. This is because his spirit has been regenerated, and now operates in the supernatural through the power of the Holy Spirit that dwells in him.

The Scriptures in Romans chapter 5:8, tell us of God's unconditional love, which says:

But God demonstrates His own love toward us, in that while we were still sinners, Christ died for us, NKJV.

God's word in Psalms 139:13-18 made us to know that He Who formed us has a special thought and plan towards us, as confirmed by the Psalmist in the above mentioned verses where he said:

*You made all the delicate, inner parts of my body, and knit them together in my mother's womb. .... You were there while I was being formed in utter seclusion! You saw me before I was born and SCHEDULED each day of my life before I began to breathe. Everyday was recorded in your book! How precious it is, Lord, to realise that You are thinking about me constantly! I cannot even count how many times a day your thoughts turn towards me.............."*TLB.

Therefore, unless people find out what God's special thoughts and plan towards them are; and what God had scheduled each day for them all through their lives, such people will continue to live in delusion, and will be playing god, or paying allegiance to an idol, other than the true God. Thus the answer revealed to David, indicates that man in his raw state is ordinary; without God's glory and honour; is just existing like an animal, without a future in God's Kingdom.

Therefore, unless man's glory and honour are restored by the second Adam, man is consigned to eternal damnation, no matter how morally sound or how benevolent man may be. Builders do not build on rots! They first clear the rot, replace the top soil and may do some piling to restore the site to a buildable standard, and after testing that it is good, they will start the foundation. So also, man must admit his short comings, clear the rot that Adam brought on us all, by accepting Jesus or rededicating his life to Jesus, before man's glory and honour are restored. It is clear from

God's word, that no man can do that by himself or his will power, no wonder Paul in Romans 7:24 cried out ...."

"Oh wretched man that I am! Who shall deliver me
from the body of this death?"

This was because he had tried all he could, and discovered he was incapable of restoring the lost glory to himself. He found that the desire to do evil was present in him - who wants to do good - thus making him a prisoner of the law of sin at work within him. He could not stop himself from doing what he does not want to do like cheating, lusting, bearing malice, envy, unforgiveness, love of money, being diplomatic with lying, cursing, anger and other abstract things that go on in his heart, which are evil and unrighteous! In our contemporary world, many have consistently made New Year resolutions, and have failed, due to man's frailty. Like David, Paul got an answer, when he said, in verse 25 of the same chapter;

"I thank God through Jesus Christ our Lord.......", I shall be delivered from the body of this death.

He then concluded that so far as he yields his mind to the Lord Jesus Christ, he will be at peace with God. He will then serve the law of God and not be in bondage to sin anymore. It is only pride of life, desire for pleasures of this world, shame of associating with Master Jesus, intellectual and spiritual arrogance that would make man, not to reach out for the restoration of man's glory and honour through Christ Jesus.

There is still time to make a "U" turn, and go back to Jesus to clear the rot in your life, forgive your sins, and restore all that needs to be restored. He is ever waiting! A song says

"He spread His hands on the cross x3,
Inviting all who desire life everlasting,
To come into His embrace"

Will you accept the invitation, as He is knocking at the door of your heart, as stated in *Revelations 3:20 which says "Behold, I (Jesus) stand at the door and knock, if any person hears My voice and opens the door (of his heart), I will come in to him and dine (fellowship) with him, and he with Me.* NKJV. Words in bracket, added by me, for emphasis.

Will you open? It is for you to decide, as it is only you that can open it, as the door handle is on the inside! May it not be too late!

CHAPTER V

There Is No Middle Ground

So then because you are lukewarm and neither
hot or cold I will spew you out of My mouth
—*Rev 3:16*

According to the scriptures, in our daily living on this earth, we are constantly faced with only two options, from which one can choose. These options are mutually exclusive, it is not "a little to the left and a little to the right"; it is either you are on the right or you are on the left. No middle course! This I believe is the way God looks at our activities on this earth, and has clearly made us to know the consequences of either of the options we select.

As in information technology, when you acquire Software and do not configure it to suit your purpose, the default parameters will be the case. The same with Biblical options, you must consciously make a choice, and declare it for all to know, whether you want to serve God or you want to live your own life. Once you do not make a decision, it means the default—the opposite of what God prescribed for us—is the case with you. Unwittingly, you have chosen to live your own life in your own way, as it seems good in your own eyes. The scriptural references below paint the picture of the two options, now let's consider the two options.

According to the Scripture, <u>broad is the way</u>—it is easy to find and many find it by default—that leads away from God; in that way everything is acceptable and everyone's "truth" is valid, based on universal love of "live and let live". Those who chose to "live once and die forever", love this way.

In this "loving" path, no one is left out, it is very liberal and accommodating—no one must condemn your bias or orientation in life. The Scripture calls it the way that seems good in one's eye! In Proverbs 16:25, we are told that

> "There is a way that seems good unto man, but the end leads to destruction".

Those who choose to travel this broad way, in order to find "fulfillment in life" to indulge their flesh, fail to realize its downward descent into destruction! It is a path without God; hence all the "good times" it gives, end in disappointment.

On the contrary, the other <u>way is narrow</u>, and very few find it; because it is not pleasing and attractive to the flesh, and diligence is needed to find it. When found, it is either you drop your ungodly habits and accept the righteous character found in Jesus Christ, or you will not enter. Those who choose to "die once and live forever" choose this narrow way, where they enter the narrow gate of faith in Christ Jesus, to find peace, love and joy of a relationship with Him.

One cannot face both directions at the same time. There must be a choice of which of the ways to take; because they lead to different eternal destinations. Also, God's word explained this with the following illustrations. One cannot drink from both cups, (the Lord's cup and the Devil's cup); or eat from both tables (the Lord's table and Satan's table). You are either carnally minded or Spiritually minded, they are all mutually exclusive! God's word in Romans 8:6 summarises it as follows: ... *to be carnally minded is death; but to be spiritually minded is life and peace.* KJV

The choice is yours; this is one thing in life, which no other person can choose for you. Making the choice is also time bound. God's word made it clear in Ecclesiastes 3:1, that there is a time and a season for everything under the Sun. My candid counsel is for you to make the choice now, based on II Corinthians 6:2, and I recommend *OPTION II*. Procrastinating or being indecisive about making this choice, means that you are by default under *OPTION 1*

Now review the Table below, it shows us from the scripture that there is no middle ground; either you are on the right or the left.

Either you are on the Lord's side or on the other—the broad way, consciously or by default. Those who choose to travel on the broad way (death) are located under Option I, on the left side of the Table; while the very few that found the narrow way are located under Option II (life) on the right side of the table.

OPTIONS	OPTION I	OPTION II	
Life and death	Death	Life	Joshua 24
Two Masters	Mammon	God	Mathew 6:24
Two Foundations	Foundation on sand	Foundation on rock	Matt 7:24-27
Two Cups,	Satan's Cup	The Lord's Cup	1 Corinth 10:21
Two Tables	Satan's table	The Lord's table	
Two Gates,	Wide gate	Narrow gate	Matt 7:13-14
Two ways	Broad way	Narrow way	
Two sons— prodigal and his brother	Elder brother	Prodigal son	Lk 15:11-32
Two sons	One who said I will do it, but did not	The one who said, I will not, but eventually did it	Matt 21:28-32
Two Systems— Tribulations and Peace	The World— Tribulations	The Word—Peace	Jn 16:33
Eternity	Hell fire, Lake of fire	Kingdom of God, Heaven	Rev 21

Old/New man	Old man	The New man	Col 3:8-10
Goats/Sheep	The Goats	The Sheep	Matt 25:32-33, 41
What fellowship hath:			II Corinth 6: 14-16
	Unrighteousness	Righteousness	
What Communion hath:			
	Darkness	Light	
What concord hath:	Belial (Baal)	Christ	
What part or portion hath			
	Unbeliever	Believer	
What agreement hath:			
	Idols	Temple of God	

In conclusion, as we reflect on what we have read in the above table, let us examine ourselves whether we have strayed to the left side, since we believed. We should know that being born again is a privilege -1 Peter 1:3. God, out of His boundless mercy gave us this privilege. Therefore, we should not misuse it or take it for granted; for nothing evil will be permitted into the City of God, the new Jerusalem. No immoral or dishonest person, ..., it is only those whose names are written in the Lamb's Book of life, Revelations 21:27. Those not permitted were described as follows in God's word—whereas outside the city are those who have strayed away from God,—the sorcerers, the idolaters, the immoral and murderers, the fearful and all those who love to lie and do lie, Revelations 22:15. Finally, the Preacher, in Ecclesiastes 12:13-14 said, Let us hear the conclusion of the whole matter, for God will bring every work of man into judgment, with every secret thing, whether it be good (option 2), or bad (option 1). He concluded that the whole duty of man is to fear God and keep His commandments or words. My own conclusion is, align with option 2, obey God's word and you will be glad, you did.

CHAPTER VI

Balanced And Un-balanced Believers

"… For he that doubts is like a wave of the sea, driven and tossed by the wind. … A double minded man is unstable in all his ways"
—James 1:6b, 8.

Depression, in my view is a symptom of life without the Life Giver—Jesus Christ. A well-functioning Christian, a balanced believer, a follower of Christ whose life is in sync with the life giver; is always filled with hope. Such a person is full of expectations that the word of God can never be broken, that it must surely come to pass, and cannot fail (Isaiah 55:8-11).Thus such a balanced believer, who is governed by the word in what he thinks on, cannot be overtaken by depression. This is because, the mind has been renewed by the word of God, as commanded in Ephesians 4:23, which says "…be renewed in the spirit of your mind", KJV. This renewal is achieved by reading, meditating and acting by faith on God's word. Thus when the evil one— Satan, your adversary comes, as a roaring lion to devour the individual with depressive thoughts, the Spirit of God on the inside, would counter such thoughts with the living word of God, that is in the person, and there would be peace. That is, as God's word explained in Isaiah 59:19; the Holy Spirit would raise a standard or defence and wipe such thoughts away.

In whatever situation, such believer will manifest like Joseph, who despite all forms of provocation, abuse, cruelty, even by his blood brothers, he was never depressed, or felt rejected by the attitude of those who were supposed to love and care for him. The foundation for this consistent character Joseph displayed throughout his ordeal, is in line with Psalms 23:4; where the Psalmist, from his Spirit inspired statement had already conditioned his mind with God's promises; this made him to emphatically say …*"Even though I walk through the valley of the shadow of death, I will fear no evil, because You God are with me"*. Truly, David weathered the storm, during his ordeal in the hands of Saul, and never got depressed. He continually encouraged himself in the Lord, I Samuel 30:6. Thus, Joseph was forgiving and plotted no revenge, against his brothers.

Why? This was because; he was of an upright heart, devoid of malice and bitterness. There is no doubt, that such a heart found in Joseph, would have been conditioned by God's word. Thus, the meditations of his heart and the words of his mouth were in all the circumstances pure, and acceptable in the sight of the Lord. His responses to those ugly and depressing situations were in sync with the following passages in God's word; which I regard as our Guideline, on how to respond and handle every depressing/ unpleasant situation. They are among others: (Words in bracket, added by me in the quotation under bullet point 3)

- **Giving of thanks in every thing**
1 Thess 5:17 says:

"In everything give thanks, for this is the will of God concerning you."

- **Do not be anxious**

Phil 4:6 says:

"Be anxious for nothing, but through prayer and supplication let your request be made known unto God,"

- **Think on things that build up your faith**

Phil 4:8 says:

"Finally my brethren, *(not matter the situation you are in or you find yourself)* think and meditate on

- whatsoever things are true,
- whatsoever things are honest,
- whatsoever things are just,
- whatsoever things are pure,
- whatsoever things are lovely,
- and whatsoever things are of good report;
- if there be any virtue, and
- if there be any praise, think on these things.

A balanced Christian should live a life of love; the kind of love found in Jesus Christ. God's word—the scriptures made us to know in I Corinthians 13:3; that whatever is done without love, profits us nothing. The word of God went further and painted a vivid picture of the characteristics of love in action. This is as shown in verses 4-8, of I Corinthians 13. These are the kind of love manifestations expected in a balanced Christian's life.

These character manifestations were also encapsulated in another form in Galatians 5:22-23, as the Fruit of the Spirit. The nine characteristics of the Fruit of the Spirit are—Love, Peace, Joy, Patience, Kindness, Goodness, Faithfulness, Gentleness, and Self-Control.

Thus, I Corinth 13:4-8 defines love in this way:

> Love suffers long
> Love is kind
> Love does not envy
> Love does not parade itself
> Love is not puffed up
> Love does not behave rudely
> Love does not seek its own
> Love is not easily provoked
> Love thinks no evil
> Love does not rejoice in iniquity
> Love rejoices in truth
> Love bears all things
> Love believes all things
> Love hopes all things
> Love endures all things
> Love never fails!

Even in the midst of agony, pain, feeling of loneliness, deprivation, feeling of being used and dumped, or what seems a hopeless situation, a well functioning Christian—the Follower of Christ, will overcome by the Spirit inspired thoughts, through giving of thanks, as noted above, and never feel abandoned. This is based on the fact that he is filled with the living word of God, and is aware of His promised presence in any situation! He is conscious of God's promises, such as—'I will never leave you nor forsake you', NKJV (Hebrews 13:5). Even when you pass through the valley of the shadow of death, He is there with you; as He was with the three Hebrew children, in the furnace (Daniel 3:24-25).

Always remember and also confess it to yourself, that God is able to do exceedingly, abundantly (immeasurably) above all that we could ask or think or imagine, according to His power that works in us (Eph 3:20). God is omnipotent – all powerful.

So also, He was with Daniel throughout his ordeal, his trials and eventual sentence to death—being fed to the lion's.

He was with me, when I was abducted in my car by four heavily armed robbers. That day, when they struck unexpectedly, the enemy wanted panic to overtake me, but the Spirit of God raised a standard, with the Blood of Jesus! I found myself pleading the Blood of Jesus three times, and I then went into silent praying in tongues. I came out unhurt, because God gave me boldness and panic ceased, I became fearless as the Holy Spirit took over, and I eventually recovered my car.

It will take the word of God in our heart, for the Spirit to raisea standard, with such declarations as — "It is written, God has not given me the spirit of fear, but of power, of love and of a sound mind", II Timothy 1:7; "It is written, I shall not die, but live to declare the goodness of the Lord, in the land of the living", Psalm 118:17; and "It is written, by His stripes, I am healed." I Peter 2:24.

To experience God's love to the fullest, have good success and be prosperous, and to avoid depression, one must "observe to do according to all that is written" in the word of God (Joshua 1:8).

Learn and ask for the grace to give thanks in all things; learn not to be anxious in anything; learn to think and meditate on whatsoever meets the criteria given above; do not lean on your own understanding.

True followers of Christ, never feel lonely, because they are indwelt by the Holy Spirit; Who guides and teaches them in every situation.

Finally sow love, ask for grace to show the Jesus kind of love always. Note, what you sow is what you reap, for God is a God of justice. Ask for His grace, to learn to sow agape love, for no one can do it by their might or power, it will take His grace and His Spirit for us to manifest such.

CHAPTER VII

Be An Example Of A Follower

"Be you therefore followers of God, as dear children."
—*Ephesians 5:1*

Paul was bold and confident enough of his Christian character, which I believe was known to all who were around him in those days, to declare in 1 Corinth 11:1, "follow me, even as I follow Jesus"; that is follow my instruction, the substance of what I say, follow my lifestyle, as I follow Christ's life style. Today, what is your life style telling others? Have you repented genuinely that you can boldly make Paul's kind of declaration, even to your children, or family members? A believer, that lives a compromising life, that their word, their preaching of the Gospel does not match their behavior or character or life style, will never have the confidence to make such a statement.

Paul said, let me be your model, as I look unto Jesus and imbibe His character. Today the Church has been modeled after the world! We now copy from the world into the Church, and spiritualize it; in dressing, in stealing, in lying, greediness, lusting, love of money, backbiting, petition writing, fornication and worship of contemporary Idols! From Hollywood, we now have

"Churchwood"! "That is Hollywood in the church". My greatest surprise is that most of our Church leaders are averting their eyes the other way, in order not to lose those members who bring fat offerings and pay big tithe! Some condone this in order to boast of having a mass choir and the biggest church membership. Thus this has shown that there are two categories of workers in the body of Christ; the hired labourers (the Compromiser) and those who are called (who preach the undiluted word of Truth, as the Gospel). The scripture says, "What shall it profit a man that he gains the whole world, and lose his own soul". Likewise, what shall it profit a pastor that he or she pastors the largest congregation on earth, drives the best SUV and go to hell fire. The tragedy in it is that, it is not only him, because due to his compromise of not preaching the undiluted word of God, he will most likely drag many liberal believers to hell fire also.

In Matt 5:14-16 Jesus Christ Our Master, specifically told us to be a model to others, both inside and outside the fold when He said

> "You are the light of the world, ... a city built unto top of the mountain cannot be hidden, ... and no one would light a lamp and put it under the table, but on a lamp stand for all to see... let your light so shine before men that they will see your good works and glorify your father in heaven".

Since we are called to be models, we are commanded, that the light of our character both in word and deed, should shine in such a transparent way to be an honest example for others to copy and follow. When your light shines (the light of your character), in any dark place devoid of godly virtues, it is illuminated; as you are a model, a pattern, a person to look unto. Do you realize that we are being watched, for different reasons; either for good or for bad. If the light emanating from us is such that blinds onlookers, then we need to repent and be converted; otherwise one will end up in hell fire. Such men of God whose light blind other men, are those who manifest the gifts of the Spirit, they wrought great miracles, but are not living a Spirit-filled life, they are lacking in the fruit of the spirit.

The call now is for one to examine one's self before it is too late. There is no repentance after death, for the Scripture said in the book of Hebrews 9:27, that it is appointed unto man once to die, after death, judgment. The book of II Timothy 2:19, tells us

> "Nevertheless the solid foundation of God stands, having this seal: " the Lord knows those who are His", and "let everyone who names the name of the Christ depart from iniquity". NKJV

Note that the foundation is the strongest part in a house, and in the house of God, Christ is the Chief corner stone, and we are all building on that foundation already laid by Christ. The above scripture made it plain that the Lord knows those "that are really building on His foundation, who are His", and cautioned that all those who call and identify with the name of the Lord Jesus, (who are building on His foundation) to depart from iniquity. It will not be a surprise today in our Churches, that there are many workers in the Church, whose names are not in God's roll, because the kind of light coming from them is blinding onlookers spiritually. In the physical, the undiscerning will regard them as strong believers, but such are just going through the motions of Christian activities! For such a believer, this is the right time, while you still have your breath, to go back to your foundation, which is where you will start to rebuild; as Peter said in Acts 4:19 "Repent and be converted..." otherwise the consequences will be terrible.

In my view, as of today, the standard of Christianity has been compromised and many elect are falling victims. With globalization and the Internet, it is getting worse. Today, one can hardly distinguish between a Christian and the non-Christian in public office- like Daniel and an ordinary person in similar office – as the light shining from the believer cannot even be seen by any, as we speak their language and dress like them, among other things. Some of us are even ashamed to proclaim our faith, unlike Daniel who his fellow Governors and Ministers knew his stand. What of the three Hebrew children, who frustrated the king's decree, by exhibiting boldly the faith they have in the God of heaven; to the extent that they told the king to his face, "that even if our God will not save us, we will not bow to this your idol".

In II Corinthians 3:1-3 we were referred to as "Epistles that people read", it states as follows from verse 2—

> "Ye are our epistle written in our hearts, known and read of all men, for as much as ye are manifestly declared to be the epistle of Christ ministered by us, written not with ink, but with the Spirit of the living God, not in tables of stone, but in fleshly tables of the heart".

If we are therefore a standard which people will use to justify their actions, will we be bold as Paul, and gladly proclaim "imitate me, do what you see me do, as I am doing what I see Christ do". Will those who imitate you, make heaven? If "no" or "not sure" is your response, then you must depart from iniquity, let iniquity be far from you; we do know that the blood of those who you are issuing ticket to hell fire, due to your lifestyle will be required of you.

CHAPTER VIII

Ultimate Destination—
Will You Get There?

"And Abram took Sarai his wife, and Lot his brother's
son..._and they went forth to go into the land of
Canaan; and into the land of Canaan they came."
—Genesis 12:5

Will you get to your God assigned destination in life or will you end up like Abraham's father, who took his entire family, with a focus and a vision to go to the land of Canaan; but alas, he was content to dwell in Haran, midway to the final destination. Not that he dwelt there, he also died there. Thus his destiny was stagnated (in Haran) and was also terminated in the same place. This is what the Scripture said about him, Abraham's father in Genesis 11:31-32 KJV.

"And Terah took Abram his son, and Lot the son of Haran his son's son, and Sarai his daughter-in-law, his son Abram's wife; and they went forth with them from Ur of the Chaldees, to go into the land of Canaan; and they came unto Haran, and dwelt there. And the days of Terah were two hundred and five years: and Terah died in Haran."

May you receive the stamina to overcome any form of weariness that brings stagnation; the discipline to overcome any form of discomfort, and may you receive from above all it takes to reach your God ordained goal for your life, as you keep heeding the counsel of the Holy Ghost, in Jesus name. May the good Lord, deliver you from any form of diversion or distraction or side attraction, that will make you lose your focus of His Kingdom, In Jesus Name.

Glory to God, Who will always accomplish His purpose, no matter mans' limitation. Thank God Terah had a son, by name Abram, who did not take no for an answer, who was a visionary, not limited by his immediate circumstances. He was a man of faith, a man of courage, a benevolent man. He was not deterred because of his father's death, he arose, took the bold step, to get to that destination, not known by him physically but by name. He took his wife, his nephew, and all their substance and those that were born in Haran, and they went forth to go into the land of Canaan, "and into the land of Canaan they came". I love this phrase in the rendition of the King James Version "and they went forth to go into the land of Canaan, and into the land of Canaan they came". My prayer for the reader of this book is that you arrive at your God ordained destination, no matter the hindrances, the side attractions, the distractions from friends or foes, and may you not stop to dwell midway to your destination, In Jesus name. May the project of your life not be abandoned or truncated, in Jesus name.

Note what the scripture said of Abraham in Genesis 12:5 KJV.

> "And Abram took Sarai his wife, and Lot his brother's
> son, and all their substance that they had gathered, and
> the souls that they had gotten in Haran; and they went
> forth to go into the land of Canaan; and into the land
> of Canaan they came."

It therefore requires our individual and collective commitment and determination, to reach our promised land as Abraham did; and not end as Terrah. On individual effort we need to be committed to the word of God and obey them, and constantly partnering with the Holy Spirit, in order to overcome. We are not perfect; neither do we have the will power, to go it alone. God in His wisdom, after He has offered His only begotten son Jesus Christ, to suffer and die for our sin, and had made the provision that as many as would accept the resurrected Jesus would be saved. Giving our life to Christ, is the commencement of our journey, as Terrah commenced, but we are required to continue in the life of righteousness, and holiness, in order to end well at our ultimate destination. Knowing the evil in the world, where the prince of this world, holds sway, God did not leave us alone, but sent the Holy Spirit, the third person of the Trinity, to guide, teach, counsel, comfort and help us to ensure we make it to the end. So how can you make it, when you do not speak the same language, with your Guide, Teacher and Counselor? That is why we had been charged to read and meditate on the word (of this language), day and night, so that when the Holy Spirit speaks to us, using the word, we will understand and obey. The same word hidden in our heart, as the Psalmist said in Psalms 119:11; will help us not to disobey God and will also constantly illuminate our path and our environment, Psalm 119:105; so that we do not stumble under the pressures of evil that abound around us, thereby ending our heavenly journey as Terrah ended, half-way.

If we do not allow ourselves to be led by the Holy Spirit, but choose to be carnally minded, in order to enjoy the pleasures of sin, we will also end up like Abraham's father, in a place of death. God's word in Romans 8:6; 13-14 and verse 1, says

> *"For to be carnally minded is death, but to be spiritually minded is life and peace. .... for if you live according to the flesh you will die; (eternal death in hell), but if by the Spirit you put to death the deeds of the body, you will live, (in the Kingdom of God). For as many as are led by the Spirit of God, these are sons of God. .... There is therefore now no condemnation to those who are in Christ Jesus, who do not walk according to the flesh, but according to the Spirit",* NKJV. The words in bracket are mine, for emphasis.

A good example for us to learn from is that of a couple who ended their heavenly journey tragically. This can be found in the New Testament, in Acts of the Apostles 5:1:11. This is about a man named Ananias and his wife Saphira, whom I believed started well, as Terrah did. However, in the process of time, as the Spirit of God moved in the early Church, some believers were stirred in the spirit to support the Church, especially in taking care of the poor among them. They sold their property and donated all the money to meet the needs of the Church. Probably, due to the recognition accorded brethren like Joseph, by their General Overseer, (who I assumed is Apostle Peter), when he sold his land and brought the whole money. This couple out of pride and ego started desiring such recognition by the General Overseer and the entire Church. They subsequently mapped out a strategy. They conceived in their mind, to do something as others did, though not led by the Spirit, but the flesh and its ego, they sold some property and brought only part of the money, claiming it was all. I am sure they were celebrated and recognised, may be with some of the excited brethren shouting "Praise the Lord!" Of course, this couple filled with pride, may have been beaming with smiles and probably waving "in thanksgiving unto the Lord" before the congregation. In that state, little did they know that we cannot hide our misdeeds, or intention from God, Hebrews 4:13 says

"And there is no creature hidden from His sight, but all things are naked and open to the eyes of Him to whom we must give account", NKJV.

God the Holy Spirit revealed every details of their intent and actions in the whole property deal to their General Overseer, who confronted them with the raw facts. There was an instant judgment, and both of them ended their heavenly race, the way carnally minded do.

Today, your Pastor or General Overseer may not know of those your lies or those misdeeds, but you cannot hide them from God Who knows every hidden thing. If you do not repent now, be ready to spend eternity outside God's kingdom – in hell fire.

Another example in the Old Testament is Gehazi in 2 Kings 5: 20- 27, who started well as Elisha's assistant, a student and apprentice prophet, but ended up a leper due to greed and lust after material things. What cost him his ministry, and eternal life in God's kingdom, were mere "two talents of Silver and two changes of garments", an equivalent of $4000.00 and two expensive robes. In addition, he lied to his master. He did not know that the Holy Spirit had revealed to his master everything he did. In verse 25, when he was asked by Elisha,

> *"Where did you go, Gehazi? He said, your servant did not*
> *go anywhere." NKJV*

Despite all he assisted Elisha to do, the miracles he witnessed under Elisha's ministry, he was still carnally minded and hooked to earthly things. There are no two ways about this, either you are spiritually minded or you are carnally minded.

In order to help us, God's word in Romans 12:2 admonish us where it says

> *"And do not be conformed to this world, (values of the world),*
> *but be transformed by the renewing of your mind, (with the*
> *word of God) that you may prove what is that good and*
> *acceptable and perfect will of God."*

Words in bracket were added by me, for clarity.

Examine yourself! Are you another Gehazi, in the making? It is time to repent, or time may run out on you, and it will be too late.

We as Believers in Christ must work and walk together, in our collective determination to help each other finish the race well. We are charged in this respect in Galatians 6:1 which says

> *"Dear brothers, if a Christian is overcome by some sin, you*
> *who are godly should gently help him back onto the right*
> *path, remembering that next time it might be one of you who*
> *is in the wrong." TLB.*

Caution! Do not be among those so called Christians, "who eat their wounded". Once a Christian brother or sister in a place of authority stumbles, they will be the first to condemn and demand for his or her head. We should on a constant basis, be encouraging and praying for those Christians, especially those in a place of political authority, that they may end well. They are there as ambassadors of the body of Christ.

Be determined to end as Abraham.

CHAPTER IX

Be Committed To God

"No one putting his hand on the plough and
looking back is fit for the kingdom of God"
— *Luke 9:62*

Are you committed to God—what have you sacrificed, to draw yourself near(er) to God? What have you given up?! Paul said, in Philippians 3:8 that he counts all things but loss, for the excellency of the knowledge of Jesus, Who is the Word of God. In James 4:8, the Scripture tells us "Draw near to God and He will draw near to you" and the only way we can draw near to God, is through His word, coupled with praise and prayer. His word is so important, that Jesus said in Mathew 4:4

> "Man shall not live by bread alone, but by every word
> that proceedeth out of the mouth of God".

It is through the Word that we get to understand God, and also know His will. It is the Word that nourishes our spirit man, hearing the Word—the message in the word—builds our faith, for it is written in the Scriptures that "faith comes by hearing, and hearing the word of God". It is the word that renews our mind to conform to that of Christ, which is what God wants. The more we conform the closer we draw to Him, and the more committed and intimate we become with our father. Romans 12:2 tells us

> "be not conformed to this world (that is, do not be like a dead fish that flows with the water current rather) be transformed by the renewing of your mind, (that is be dead to the world and its values, but alive unto God through His word that renews your mind) that ye may prove what is that good, and acceptable, and perfect will of God".

As we continue to renew our mind, (we will continue to swim against the water current of worldly values, systems, and traditions of men). Thus living a righteous and sanctified life; this may attract persecution. But the key thing in it is not the persecution, but that your light is shinning before all men, as Jesus commanded in Matthew 5:16

> "Let your light so shine before men, that they may see your good work and glorify your father which is in heaven".

Also there is growth through the reading and meditation on the word of God, and as one grows, it means drawing nearer and closer to God; the voice of God becomes clearer. As a believer, it helps you to overcome one of the biggest problems most of us face; the problem of our carnal desires overriding God's voice. Most often, we are so crowded with thoughts(voices) as to figure out what to do under uncertain circumstances. It is only, when we get it wrong, that one would say comments like this "something told me not to do this, this way". That "something" is the Holy Spirit speaking, through your conscience, which is voice of the Spirit. That was why Jesus said of a transformed heart "*If your heart did not condemn you, neither will I condemn you*".

We can learn from Moses' encounter with God in the bush (Exodus 3:2). He was tending the sheep of his father-in-law and was so filled with his own desires and thoughts that he could not discern God was speaking to him. That is, he was so noisy with his desires, strategizing and clamoring how to find fulfillment in life, having had to run as a fugitive earlier. Maybe he was filled with thoughts of what would become of his future, that he had completely shut out God! In order to "capture" or get his attention, God had to cause a bush to burn, without being consumed. That unbelievable-spectacular scene was then able, to halt and silence all the noise, and other things going on in his mind and around him. This caused him to draw near to observe what was happening, and thus was able to hear God. This is God, Who had been speaking all these while, without his hearing.

Has your business, your work, your family, your passion or your position in the society, made you so busy, that you are now like Moses in the wilderness as a shepherd? May you receive the wisdom to have a balance between your time and that which you devote to God, and the unction to hear God, as He speaks for our own good on daily basis, in Jesus name. Amen!

We need to deliberately set aside everything else, and take time to be in His presence, to listen to Him; it will help us find out His will for our life. It will eliminate a lot of delays, heartbreaks, and disappointments we would have experienced in life. Some believers call this taking time in His presence—Quiet time. Robert Tilton had this to say in one of his writings

> "If the children of Israel had listened to God, in the first place, they would not have wandered for forty years... If you, like the children of Israel, listen to other things instead of God, you will choke out His Word, dull your ability to hear His voice, and fall. Don't let the cares of your life, keep you from hearing God. When you take time to listen, God will prosper you 'like a tree planted by the rivers of water' and you will be blessed in whatever you do because God only asks you to do things that will succeed. Psalm 1:1-3."

We cannot draw near to God anyhow; that is on our own terms. That is why the Scriptures admonishes us, to "clean our hands—(stop stealing, fighting, drinking, smoking and all the evil we do with it), and purify our hearts—(of all the evil that are conceived in the heart)", otherwise any effort to draw nearer to God would amount to ritual, and would be of no consequence. You **CANNOT** be a sinning saint, and think you can draw nearer to God by your outward activities and services, it would not work. The foul odor of your secret dirty life, will repel the Spirit of God. However, if we cleanse our hands and purify our hearts, as commanded, and keep drawing nearer, we will come to a point of abiding in Him always. When we get to this stage, we will start experiencing a new dimension of relationship with the Father, through Jesus Christ.

In John 15:1-5, Jesus said

> "... I am the true Vine, and my Father is the Vine-Dresser... I am the Vine, you are the branches. He who abides in Me, and I in Him, bears much fruit; for without Me, you can do nothing... If anyone does not abide in Me, he is cast out as a branch and ... they are gathered and thrown into the fire, and they are burned".

This profound statement of Jesus Christ, summarizes it all; that some in the Church, who are abiding based on their own standards, values, and lifestyle, would end up, knowingly or unknowingly being cast into eternal damnation, away from the kingdom of God, which they believed they have labored for.

On the other hand, as one keeps reading, meditating on the word, and putting them into action, as in Joshua 1:8 and 1 Timothy 4:15-16. These instructions below, among others in the word will start the transformation work and one will start to have a closer walk with God:

- Be anxious for nothing, but through prayer and supplications let your request be made known unto God... Philippians 4:6
- Be slow to speak, quick to hear and slow to wrath, James 1:19
- Be angry and do not sin, do not let the sun go down before your anger, Ephesians 4:26.
- fear not, *I am with you,* for I have redeemed you, I have called you by your name; you are mine. When you pass through the waters *of affliction,* I will be with you; and

through the rivers *of problems,* they will not overflow you: when you walk through the fire *of persecution,* it shall not burn you; neither shall the flame consume you, Isaiah 43:1-5. Italicized words added by me, for clarity.

- Give, it shall be given unto you, in full and overflowing measure, pressed down, shaken together to make room for more, and running over. For whatever measure you use to give, will be used to measure what will be given back to you. Luke 6:38

- Do not revenge, for vengeance is mine, say the Lord, Romans 12:19.

- Love your enemies, pray for those who persecute you, Mathew 5:44.

- Bless them that curse you, Mathew 5:44.

- Do not think of yourself so highly; rather prefer others to yourself, Romans 12:10.

- Pray without ceasing, do not give up, no matter the situation, 1Thess 5:17; Luke 18:1.

- Quench not the Holy Spirit, but be led by the Spirit, Ephesians 4:30; 1Thess 5:19; Romans 8:14

- Give thanks in everything, for this is the will of God concerning you, I Thess 5:18.

- Keep "looking unto Jesus, the Author and Finisher of our faith", Heb 12:2.

Recognizing that Christ is the link (Ladder or Staircase) between us and heaven above (John 14:6), where He is seated at the right hand of God, interceding for us. We should explore our new relationship with God, through prayers and watching. This "staircase relationship" is also represented with the "vertical" of the cross, linking those who believe. To have free access to it, so that you can go up and down the staircase, you must be permanently attached to the True Vine, Jesus Christ. In John 15:1-5, He said, "without me you can do nothing", hence without your dependence on Him, you cannot have the unction, to climb up and down! You can only reach out to Him, and depend on Him through His word. Through His word, we get insight of Who He is, what He wants us to do, how, when, and where; and finally what resources He has made available to enable us do it.

Christ is the Link between us and others in our relationship (this represents the "horizontal" of the cross). Any relationship, not linked through the love of Christ will not be peaceful, smooth and may not last. It will be full of suspicion, animosity, deceit, selfishness; instead of selflessness, love, sacrifice, and integrity.

We cannot be talking of a closer walk, with the Lord, while we are living in unforgiveness, malice, backbiting, and not in terms with our neighbours. Jesus said, if you are bringing your offering, and you remember, your brother has a case with you, it is better you keep that offering, and go first and reconcile with him, before giving your offering. With our current disposition, in most of our relationships, it would imply that most of our relationships, it would mean that most of our offerings were not acceptable unto God. Even our tithes, and donations. Ask God for His great grace, to forgive and to make peace with others.

If you are in the negative habit of unforgiveness; that from time to time you regurgitate the memories of all the "so called wrongs" relish them, and may act on them in your relationship with the person (this is especially terrible between spouses); then hear the conclusion of the whole matter, as our Master Jesus said in

Matthew 18:23-35, in the parable of the king who wanted to settle accounts with his servants; and there was one of the servants who was unable to pay what he owed. So the king ordered that he be sold with his household and belongings so that payment could be made. When the servant discovered what was about to befall him, he fell down and pleaded. On compassionate grounds, the king forgave him, wrote off his entire debt, and he was released to freedom. However, he failed to extend the same compassionate gesture to his fellow servant; he became mean and violent in the manner which he demanded for the immediate payment of the little sum owed him. To his un-doing, the king heard what he did, and he was promptly re-arrested and delivered to tormentors until he could pay all the debts he owed. The New King James renders it this way in Matthew 18:34-35

> "And the master was angry and delivered him to torturers until he should pay all that was due to him."

And Jesus said in verse 35

> "So My heavenly Father also will do to you if each of you from his heart, does not forgive his brother his trespasses".

You may be suffering from tormentors in your present ordeal; and you are fasting and praying, binding and casting. You are going nowhere, unless you comply with verse 35.

CHAPTER X

Life-style Gospel

"So be careful how you act, these are difficult
days. Don't be fools, be wise".
—*Ephesians 5:15 (TLB)*

We have been put in trust with the gospel as noted in this Scripture—

> "But as we were allowed of God to be put in trust with the gospel, even so we speak; not as pleasing men, but God, which tries our hearts".
>
> 1 Thessalonians 2:4.

So standing as occasion demands before men, preaching the gospel is ordained by God, before hand, and not of our own making, for He alone orders our step.

Message—examine your ways, for surely we will give account sooner or later? Your ways may seem good in your own eye, but where does it lead you? Is it to the right or to the left?

To the right means you are finding fulfillment in life, in accordance with the Scriptures, the word of God, the true gospel; however, to the left, means away from God; based on the way that seems good in your own eyes, in your own reasoning, counting on your own maturity and independence. But note that any life, being lived independent of God through our Lord Jesus Christ is a wasted one that will be full of regrets at the end.

In Proverbs 21:2 and 16:25 the word of God says

> "every way of man is right in his own eyes; but the
> Lord weighs the heart; there is a way that seems good
> unto man, but the end leads to destruction".

In Psalms 139:1-18, the word of God made us to know that God knows every of our thoughts, our locations—wherever we are, whatever we are doing—thus we cannot hide from Him; and He equally knows what is good for us. Therefore, do not allow yourself, to rewrite what God has already written about you, which is for your own good. This passage made it plain that one cannot hide from God, darkness, distance, cannot hide you from God. Why? This is because the word of God made us to know that God is Omniscience—All Knowing; Omnipotent—all Powerful; and Omnipresence—Everywhere; above all He created you. We should be aware that we have a short time here on earth, and that we are all aging by the day, and slowly but continuously going towards our end on this earth; every step we take as we walk, takes us closer to our grave. Also we should realize that each minute, each hour, each day that passes, the number of minutes, hours, days we have left on this earth is reduced. The knowledge of all these should kindle us to consider our way of life, and not be deceived that we have much time, or that we want to enjoy life now and later repent, hence we stick to those ways that are taking us afar from God, our creator.

The Scriptures, says in James 4:4,

> "Ye adulterers and adulteresses, know ye not that the friendship of the world is enmity with God? Whosoever therefore will be a friend of the world is the enemy of God".

While 1 Corinthians 1:18 made us to know that

> "… the preaching of the cross (gospel of Jesus) is to them that perish foolishness; but unto us which are saved it is the power of God.
>
> It is foolishness to them, because of approaching the gospel with human wisdom, arrogance, intellectual reasoning and logic!"

It noted that such lack the knowledge of the word of God, and thus they continue in their folly. In the same chapter in verse nineteen, the Scripture tells us the mind of God where He said

> "… I will destroy the wisdom of the wise, (of this world) and will bring to nothing the understanding of the prudent".

Who are the prudent of this world and who are the wise? They are the movers and shakers of any society, whose beliefs are governed by the value system of the world—the end justifies the means. Thus any approach adopted in finding fulfillment for their passions, namely; lust for power, with the accompanying ego, pride, and self conceit; love for money, recognition, sex and its pleasures, and for whatever else the individual desires, is acceptable.

It is my submission that this is the root of war and fighting everywhere; violence, destruction, and all forms of conflicts, are as a result of man trying to find fulfillment in life, without Jesus Our Saviour. The Scriptures in James 4:1-3, asked a series of questions to this effect;

> "From whence come wars and fighting among you?
> Come they not hence, even of your lusts that war in
> your members? Ye lust, and have not: ye kill, and
> desire to have, and cannot obtain: ye fight and war,
> yet ye have not, because ye ask not. Ye ask, and receive
> not, because ye ask amiss, that ye may consume it
> upon your lusts".

The rich man in Luke 16:25-31 tried it, he found what seems to be fulfillment with his wealth, while on earth, but suddenly turned to be an Evangelist, while in hell fire. He asked father Abraham to send Lazarus to go to the earth, to his father's house and tell his five brothers to listen to the prophets, because he is in a place of torment! A place of anguish he will remain forever—no coming out! You may not read from me again, but that which the Lord laid in my heart I have done through this book, as commanded in Ezekiel 3:16-21; which says, " .... The word of the Lord came to me, saying, ..."When I say to the wicked, 'you shall surely die', and you give him no warning, nor speak to warn the wicked (the sinner) from his wicked (sinful) way, to save his life, that same wicked (sinful) man shall die in his iniquity; but his blood I will require at your hand. "Yet, if you warn the wicked (sinner) and he does not turn from his wickedness (sinfulness), nor from his wicked (sinful) way, he shall die in his iniquity; but you have delivered your soul". Again, when a righteous man turns from his righteousness and commits iniquity, and I lay a stumbling block before him, he shall die, because you did not give him warning, he shall die in his sin, and his righteousness which he has done shall not be remembered; but his blood I will require at your hand. "Nevertheless if you warn the righteous man that the righteous should not sin, and he does not sin, he shall surely live because he took warning; also you will have delivered your soul," NKJV. *The words in bracket are mine, for a better understanding.* I am free of any man's blood.

Today, many young men who knew the Word of God, abruptly walked away from the Lord, as a result of lust as noted above. They have unwittingly become independent. How can a branch be independent from a tree and survive? While some think they will find fulfillment in life by indulging in pleasures that abound in the world, to gratify the flesh, or amass all the wealth they can, for posterity! At the end of it all, at the close of their life, they will discover it is all vanity. The Preacher, King Solomon—the wisest human ever lived, summarized it as follows; 'vanity upon vanity, all is vanity, pursuing after the wind!' That is life without Jesus! It is vanity, at the end. What shall it profit a man that he gains the whole world and loose his soul.

One should learn from Peter's experience and encounter, during the trial of the Lord Jesus Christ, before His crucifixion. He was before now very close to Jesus, but at His arrest he followed his Lord and Master at a distance, Luke 22:54-55. As they drew near the courtyard gate of the High Priest, he went closer but not to the Master. When they entered Palace of the High Priest (a place of pleasure), he completely cut off himself from His master, and joined the world (the servants of the prince of this world) to enjoy the warmth of the fire side(pleasing the flesh)!

> "And Peter followed him afar off, even into the palace of the high priest: and he sat with the servants, and warmed himself at the fire"
>
> —Mark 14:54

Where am I now, is the question you should ask yourself, am I in the palace (of the prince of this world) already, by my life style?

Your own warmth of the fire side, could be in the bosom of a strange woman or man; it could be in the alcohol bar or gay bar, or pornographic site you visit, or those fraudulent and ungodly behaviours you indulge in, or the idol of making money, stealing, cheating, or that your work or business has become your Idol/god. Is your fireside in the occult, while professing to be a Christian or constant visit to demonic shrines/mediums? Whatever is that warmth, beware that that fire side will not last forever, the day it will go off is by the corner; and thereafter, the question time will come!

Better come out now, before it will be too late. Peter, had an opportunity to reconsider his ways, when a young maid, questioned him and said, "were you not one of them?"

> "And a maid saw him again, the second time and
> began to say to them that stood by, this is one of them."
> —Mark 14:69.

Note this he denied it, though his denial gave him a temporal relief. He ran away to another corner, and was confronted by the same situation, for the third time, if not that he repented, wept and asked for forgiveness, he would have gone like Judas Iscariot, who committed suicide! Do not for this temporary pleasure ruin your eternity; in hell fire.

CHAPTER XI

"God" Of Man

"But he who glories, let him glory in the Lord".
—*II Corinthians 10:17*

Are you baptized in the Holy Spirit, speak in tongues, prays and sings in tongues, but you do not live a spirit-filled life; then you are living a wasted Christian life. A spirit-filled life is a Christ-like life, a life of faith, righteousness and holiness. The Scripture in I Corinthians 12:8-10 and Gal 5:22-23 enumerated the attributes that can be found in a Spirit-filled life. These are in two compartments, namely the gifts of the Spirit and the fruit of the Spirit; thus to live a spirit-filled life there must be a balanced manifestation of both, in such a life. But alas! Today, any man that manifests the gift of the Spirit is regarded as a spirit-filled, anointed man of God; whereas, such are lacking in the fruit of the Spirit. They are almost void of Christ-likeness.

That is why Jesus said in Mathew 7:21-24, that such men of God would come in the last days, but He would reject them, despite their references to exploits and miraculous manifestations in their ministries during their time on earth. They were busy shining with the gift of the Spirit, and at the same time living in iniquity, forgetting that the gift of God is without repentance. Thus, they equate the working of miracles, the exercise of the gifts of the Spirit to godliness. The Scriptures made it clear in I Corinthians 13, that no matter the extent we manifest the gifts of the Spirit—that we can even raise the death, give our bodies to be burnt—but we lack the fruit of the Spirit, that it profits us nothing in the Kingdom of God. Such a person, such man of God is like a sounding cymbal and a noisy gong. We tend to neglect and grossly overlook the weightier fruit of the Spirit! Almost everybody in our generation is clamoring for the power ministry that will advertise them, make them known, popular, and rich; that most often some cross the line of sharing God's glory. It is now common to hear men of God, use such phrase as - "my church", and they love being referred to and introduced as "Founder and General Overseer, worldwide"

Now I ask which Church are they the founder of? The Church of Jesus Christ! Which Jesus Himself said *"I will build my Church and the gates of hell would not prevail"*

In my view, any Christian that lacks in any aspect of the fruit of the Spirit is carnal and condemnation is awaiting them. I am sure that is why we are commanded in Gal 5:16 to

> "Walk in the Spirit, so that you will not fulfill the
> lust of the flesh, for those who fail to do so, shall not
> inherit the Kingdom of God"

Whereas Romans 8:1, (KJV) puts it clearly and without doubt, where it says—

"There is now no condemnation for those who are
in Christ Jesus, who walk not after the flesh but after
the Spirit."

This means that there is condemnation for those who are born
again, speaks in tongues, work miracles, etc, but do not walk after
the Spirit, to live a Spirit—filled life. Why? They lack the fruit
of the Spirit. The nine spiritual characteristics work together as
one—hence no option to pick and choose which one to be formed
in you. The nine facets or virtues of the fruit of the spirit, which
are expected to be formed in us, are:

Love—unconditional love, no strings attached.
Joy—not affected by circumstances, can be experienced in the
    midst of suffering; an inward satisfaction from the Holy Spirit,
    that God is sovereign and in control of all situations.
Peace—the peace of God that pass all understanding
Long suffering—Patience
Gentleness—mild temper, calm spirit
Goodness—kindness
Faithfulness—trustworthy or dependable
Meekness—humility, humble—both inwardly and outwardly
Temperance—Self-Control, moderation

However, one should have this in mind, that spiritual gifts and
fruit of the Spirit have no meaning unless motivated by love.
Any man of God, manifesting all these, would not be expected
to manifest the works of the flesh, listed in Galatians 5:19-21.
These works are so dirty, so filthy to be associated with believers,
or with men of God. For a quick reference to the listed works of
the flesh, they are:

Adultery

Fornication

Uncleanness (Filthy thoughts)

Lasciviousness (shameful deeds, lustfulness,…)

Idolatry (includes anything which one passionately gives affection above God)

Witchcraft (spiritism, magical arts, casting spells and charms,…)

Hatred (rooted bitterness, malice, ill-will..)

Emulation (jealousy,..)

Wrath (deep rooted anger,..)

Strife (contention, quarreling,…)

Seditions (divisions, factions, stirring up strife,…)

Heresies (wrong doctrine,..)

Envying

Murders (includes spoken words, that can kill ones' spirit, or may lead to death)

Drunkenness

Reveling (Wild Parties)

The Scriptures admonished us not to judge, Mathew 7:7, but the same Scriptures asked us to examine ourselves, to know whether we are still in faith. In other words, we are asked to judge ourselves, using the word of God as our yardstick. In the light of this, we can prepare a Balanced-Score Card, to evaluate ourselves to see how far we faired. We are going to use the fruit of the Spirit, Gifts of the Spirit and works of the flesh as attributes in our score-cards.

	Attributes	YES	NO	NOT SURE
	Born Again			
	Filled with the Holy Spirit			
	Manifests the gifts of the Holy Spirit			
	Fruit of the Spirit—now the test is here answer "Yes" or "No" or "Not sure"			
	Love—Does your character, life style show the God's kind of unconditional love?			
	Joy—do you radiate the joy of the Lord, in all circumstances, even when in the valley?			
	Peace—Are you a peace maker, do you radiate peace around you?			
	Patience—are you patience with people and with God, when your expectations from them are not met			
	Gentleness—Are you gentle inwardly and outwardly, of a calm spirit, mild temper.			
	Goodness—are you of a noble character, righteous and good to others. Are you kind?			
	Faithfulness—Are you trustworthy, integrity driven and truthful?			
	Meekness—Are you unassuming, humble, lowly?			
	Self Control—Moderation, in every situation, as occasion demands?			
	WORKS OF THE FLESH—Am I associated with or can it be found in me?			
	Adultery			
	Fornication			
	Uncleanness (Filthy thoughts)			

Lasciviousness (shameful deeds, lustfulness,…)			
Idolatry (includes anything which one passionately gives affection above God)			
Witchcraft (Spiritism, magical arts, casting spells and charms,…)			
Hatred (rooted bitterness, malice, ill-will..)			
Emulation (jealousy,..)			
Wrath (deep rooted anger,..)			
Strife (contention, quarreling,…)			
Seditions (divisions, factions, stirring up strife,…)			
Heresies (wrong doctrine,..)			
Envying (being covetous; greedy)			
Murders (includes spoken words, that can kill ones' spirit, or may lead to death)			
Drunkenness			
Reveling (Wild Parties)			

CHAPTER XII

Jesus Baptism—Lessons/Insights

'Go therefore and make disciples of all nations,
baptizing them in the name of the Father,
and of the Son, and of the Holy Spirit"
—*Matthew 28:19*

Baptism is a symbolic action, it may appear ordinary, but it has a deep implication, in our Christian faith. I mean immersion baptism.

If it has no deep implication, Jesus would not have subjected Himself, to be baptized. He did it to show us His followers, an example. Moreover as we do it, it shows our public declaration for Jesus; telling the whole world that our old man—our sinful nature—had been buried with Christ, and a new man, renewed in Christ has emerged. It is also a sign of humility, to subject oneself to water baptism by immersion, on the part of the followers!

This informed what played out between John the Baptist and Jesus Christ in Matthew chapter 3; when Jesus requested John to baptize Him. This request to John looked awkward to him, that he objected. —

But John kept objecting and said, "I ought to be baptized by you. Why have you come to me? Jesus answered, "For now this is how it should be, because we must do all God wants us to do." Then John agreed.

So Jesus was baptized. And as soon as he came out of the water, the sky opened, and he saw the Spirit of God coming down on him like a dove, Matthew 3:14-16 CEV.

Note that John objected, to baptizing Jesus, and said out of respect, that it should be the other way round. Also note Jesus response, which resolved the whole matter—John "For now this is how it should be, because we must do all God wants us to do". Human protocols and procedures could be a hindrance, and would negate the will of God, thus quench the Holy Spirit!

Lessons of "doing all God wants us to do, attract open heavens"; "note it says "all" not "some". Thus in verse 16, it says

> "As soon he came out of the water, (in total obedience),
> the sky (heavens) opened, unto Him! The Holy Spirit
> descended, and alighting unto Him, the voice of the
> Lord came forth audibly 'This is my beloved Son in
> Whom I am well pleased'"

Brethren, no amount of sacrifice, working of miracles, prayers, and your service unto the Lord will take the place of obedience! Obedience opens doors, breaks yokes, brings healing, preserves life, restores life, brings increase, and victory, among other virtues!

Naaman obeyed and got healed, after being persuaded to dip himself in Jordan river seven times; 2 Kings 5:9-14. In Luke 5:4-7, Peter obeyed after some argument that he has fished all night and discarded his professional experience, launched into the deep, and there was a big haul of fishes!

In Acts 9:10-18, Ananias obeyed to go and lay hands on Saul of Tarsus (Paul) after putting up some resistance, which fear brought upon him, having known Paul's evil antecedents; and God used him to liberate the greatest evangelist, teacher, philosopher lawyer, preacher, and Apostle, whom God used to author most of the New testament. The man who was bold to say "imitate me as I imitate Christ," I Corinthians 11:1; I wonder who among us today would be bold enough to make such a statement. One would observe that these three men (Naaman, Peter and Ananias) did not just obey, they asked questions, probably to clear their doubts, fears, or for clarification, but the important thing to note is that they obeyed, without much delay.

Compare them with the encounter between John the Baptist and Jesus, they are similar. John did not jump into baptizing Jesus immediately; he resisted, but later obeyed, thus fulfilling his ministry. Thus, it is not sin, for us to ask questions, when prompted; however asking questions should not occasion delay; as this would amount to delayed obedience, which may amount to disobedience.

On the other hand, Joshua when called obeyed, without any question, when he was asked to go and take Jericho! He was patience enough (long suffering) to obey and carryout the "cumbersome" instructions to the letters, as contained in Joshua

6:2-4; 11-16; 20. They the children of Israel, with Joshua their leader, marched round the wall of Jericho patiently, Thirteen times. They did this once a day in the first six days, and on the seventh day, seven times. They endured and the fact that *they did all that the Commander of the Lord's army asked them to do*, their total obedience gave them open heaven and there was victory, in an unprecedented manner. Most often, impatience causes us (men of God) to disobey the will of God. Patience is a virtue one must cultivate. See Galatians 5:22-23a, the fruit of the Spirit.

What of Joseph, Jesus earthly father, he obeyed in several instances, and thus through him, the will of God for mankind was fulfilled and was not truncated by the Satan. One he obeyed in not putting Mary away, as recorded in Mathew 1:19-21; 24-25, which says:

> *"Then Joseph her husband, being a just man, and not wanting to make her a public example, was minded to put her away secretly. But while he thought about these things, behold, an angel of the Lord appeared to him in a dream, saying, "Joseph, son of David, do not be afraid to take to you Mary your wife, for that which is conceived in her is of the Holy Spirit. And she will bring forth a Son, and you shall call His name Jesus, for He will save His people from their sins." ....Then Joseph, being aroused from sleep, did as the angel of the Lord commanded him and took to him his wife, and did not know her till she had brought forth her firstborn Son. And he called His name Jesus," NKJV.*

He also obeyed when he was asked to flee with the baby and the mother to Egypt, to avoid being killed by Herod, and also that the Scriptures may be fulfilled, recorded in Mathew 2:13-15; 19-20 which reads:

> *"Now when they had departed, behold, an angel of the Lord appeared to Joseph in a dream, saying, "Arise, take the young Child and His mother, flee to Egypt, and stay there until I bring you word; for Herod will seek the young Child to destroy Him." When he arose, he took the young Child and His mother by night and departed for Egypt, and was there until the death of Herod that it might be fulfilled which was spoken by the Lord through the prophet, saying, "Out of Egypt I called My Son." Now when Herod was dead, behold, an angel of the Lord appeared in a dream to Joseph in Egypt, saying, "Arise, take the young Child and His mother, and go to the land of Israel, for those who sought the young Child's life are dead." NKJV*

Joseph in all the instances, did not argue, or ask questions, but acted in complete obedience; thus........preserved lives, caused the word of God to be fulfilled, and God's salvation plan for mankind to be accomplished.

In my view, depending on the circumstances of each encounter and your state, it may play out either way, but one must never allow any delay, as I had earlier noted. A close study of what transpired between Jesus Christ and His disciples would reveal to you, that in all cases, they did all that the Lord Jesus asked them to do, and they achieved great and outstanding results, in each of them. Most often these instructions may look foolish and out of place, but they are spiritually sound and full of the wisdom.

In the miracle of feeding five thousand men recorded in the gospel of Luke chapter 9:12-17; He gave them instruction, and said, "You give them something to eat", which by all human standards looked ridiculous. This was after the disciples demanded the He send the multitudes away, as there was no food to feed them in that solitary place. When He told them to give them something to eat, I believe He knew that they do not have more than five loaves and two fish. The brief dialogue that followed culminated in the disciples obeying His instructions. *They did all that He asked them to do,* which included arranging the people in groups of fifty. This translated to a minimum of hundred groups, because women and children were not included in the five thousand.

What happened during the sharing was spectacular. Heaven opened and the five loaves and two fish, were multiplying in the hands of the apostles, as they shared. The end result was that, food enough to feed 12 families was left over, after more than five thousand people ate and were filled.

In another instance recorded in the gospel of Luke chapter 10:1-20; when Jesus wanted to send 70 of His disciples out for evangelism. He sent them in twos, with specific instructions not to take any money with them, not carry any bag, nor take extra pair of sandals or greet anybody on the way. This set of instructions in verse 4, apart from those in verses 5 -11, looked queer; yet there were no questions from the disciples. *They expressly obeyed Him, and the purpose of sending them out was achieved. "They reached their destination".*

The testimonies that followed were stories of crushing defeat to Satanic Kingdom. They shared their exploits in the field with joy, "how demons were subject to us in Your name." After listening, Jesus said to them in verses 18-20:

"I saw Satan fall like lightening from heaven. Behold, I give you the authority to trample on serpents and scorpions, and over all the power of the enemy, and nothing shall by any means hurt you. Nevertheless do not rejoice in this, that the spirits are subject to you, but rather that rejoice because your names are written in heaven." NKJV

The ultimate joy in this was that they experienced open heaven, *because they did all that their Master asked them to do*; and also He told them to rejoice because their "names are written in heaven".

You want to attract open heaven; then live and <u>do all that God wants you to do</u>, at the right time, and that is achievable, when one is continually led by the Holy Spirit; that is being sensitive to the Holy Spirit; that lives within us. We should not allow traditions, protocols, and argument in the name of dialogue to hinder the plan of God.

CHAPTER XIII

The Ministry of Reconciliation

Now all things are of God, Who has reconciled
us to Himself, through Jesus Christ, and has
given us The Ministry of Reconciliation.
That is, God was in Christ reconciling the world to Himself...
and has committed to us the word of reconciliation."
—*II Corinthians 5:18-19*

Jesus through His death and shedding of His blood abolished our eternal separation from God; he opened the door of reconciliation for all men unto God. He also broke the wall of partition, between the Jews and the Gentiles, that means the enmity has been destroyed. This can be seen illustrated in the sketch below, based on Ephesians chapter 3.

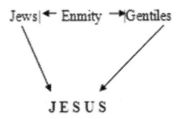

Made one by Jesus:—Children of God; Joint Heirs with Christ; Temple of the Holy Spirit; Sons of God, Born again by the living word of God.

Based on Colossians chapter 1, He made a way for all to be reconciled to God, as illustrated below.

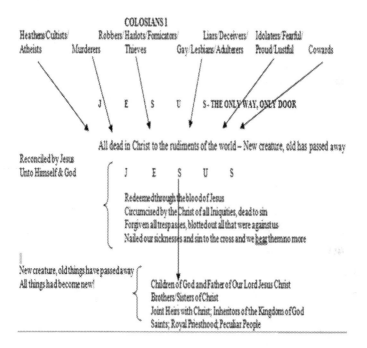

Dear reader, from the above God had made a provision for all to be reconciled to Him, through Jesus Christ. As the Scripture says

"For God so loved the world that He gave His only begotten son, that whosoever believes in Him will not perish but have eternal life;… As many as received Him, gave he power to become sons of God" John 3:16, 1:12

Thus, the only thing that will send you to hell fire is not your sin, not your past, no matter how terrible they are, it is your saying "No!" to Jesus. It is only if you refuse to accept His finished work on the cross of Calvary, and invite Him into your life to be your Master and Saviour, that your ultimate destination will be outside His kingdom. The Scripture says in the book of

II Corinthians 6:2

> "...behold now is the accepted time ...behold, now is
> the day of salvation",

The ball is in your court, it is for you to play it or leave it! There are only two options, either you confess your sin and say yes to Jesus, or you say no by default and face the horrible eternal consequences. You cannot be indifferent, there is no middle ground!

In conclusion, I am sure you have read and understood the truth; the decision is yours, whichever way you decide to pitch your tent, hear the conclusion of the message of reconciliation in

Revelations 22:11 which says

> "Let him who is evil (unjust) continue to do evil
> still, and him who is filthy, let him continue to be
> filthy still; let him that is righteous continue to do
> righteously; and he that is holy, let him be holy still"...
> I (Jesus) am coming quickly ...To give every man
> according to his work."

And Matthew 25:31-46 which also says

> "When the Son of Man comes in His glory; and all the
> holy angels with Him, then He will sit on the throne
> of His glory, 'All nations will be gathered before Him,
> and He will separate them one from another, as a
> shepherd divides his sheep from the goats. And He
> will set the sheep on His right hand, but the goats on
> the left. Then the King will say to those on His right
> hand, 'Come, you blessed of My Father, inherit the
> kingdom prepared for you from the foundation of the
> world'... Then He will also say to those on the left
> hand, 'Depart from Me, you cursed, into everlasting
> fire prepared for the devil and his angels.... And these
> will go away into everlasting punishment, but the
> righteous into eternal life", NKJV."

From the above Scriptures, you will understand that on the
judgment day, it is either you are on the right hand side of the
Lord, or you are on the left hand side. Now, you have the chance
to make a choice on which side you want to be. My candid advice
is, never be caught on the left hand side of our Lord Jesus. Do not
be among the goats that will be 'cast into everlasting fire, prepared
for the devil and his angels'. Rather make a decision now, invite
Jesus into your life by confessing and accepting Him as your Lord
and personal Saviour, as the word of God says in Romans 10:9-
10. Live righteously, that is, always do what meets God's approval
and be among the sheep He will set on His right hand, when He
comes in His glory.